A Funny Thing Happened on My Way through the Bible

by Martha Bolton

HONOR BOOKS
TULSA, OKLAHOMA

A Funny Thing Happened on My Way through the Bible

ISBN 1-56292-579-2

Published by Honor Books
P.O. Box 55388
Tulsa, Oklahoma 74155

Second printing, over 15,000 in print.

Introduction

The Bible is full of so many wonderful stories—stories that lend themselves to great sermons, terrific epic motion pictures, fascinating documentaries, and yes, even funny anecdotes.

This book is about the laughter that can be found within its pages. God does have a sense of humor. He once made a donkey talk. That's pretty funny. He closed the Red Sea on the Egyptian army as they pursued Moses. He had to have enjoyed that last laugh. And He stopped the builders of the Tower of Babel, the biggest project of its time, right in their tracks by confusing their languages. That scene had to have been pretty funny, too.

Always respectful of the message of the Bible, the following is meant purely for your enjoyment. May you laugh, may you learn, and may we all never forget the wealth of stories found within the pages of the greatest Book ever written.

Martha Bolton

Dedication

To Eunice, my niece,
whose laughter can lighten any situation.

Birth Announcement

It's a BIG one!

Name:	Goliath
Born:	Last Monday . . . Tuesday . . . and Wednesday
Weight:	Broke the scale
Nursery Theme:	World Wrestling Federation
Gift Suggestions:	Baby barbells
	Barbed-wire teething ring
	Junior boxing gloves
	Steel-belted playpen
	Cradle with crane lift attachment

Please, no slingshots. Baby seems to have an aversion to them.

5

Remarks made by the first Egyptians on the scene of the parting of the Red Sea:

"Whoa, dude, now *that's* a wave!"

"Me follow them? *You* follow them!"

"Sure, it's impressive,
but it kinda takes the sport out of fishing,
doesn't it?"

"I just wanna know one thing.
How are we going to word this in our report to Pharaoh?"

"Don't those people *ever* use a bridge?"

Lazarus' Funeral Folder

IN MEMORY OF ...

Deceased: Lazarus

Date of Death: Four days ~~ago~~

~~Interment:~~   ~~Be~~thany

~~Served~~ by: Sisters, Mary and Martha

"**Never mind**"

The family of Lazarus wishes to thank you
for your attendance at the funeral of our brother.

Change of Address

FOR:	<u>Adam and Eve</u>
OLD ADDRESS:	<u>Garden of Eden</u>
NEW ADDRESS:	<u>The Garden of Eden Suburbs</u>
REASON FOR MOVE:	_____ Downsizing
	_____ Too old to care for garden
	_____ Career advancement
	_____ Paradise isn't what it used to be.
	__X__ Evicted

DIRECTIONS TO NEW HOME: <u>Proceed the same as to the old address, only just before you get to the garden, hang a left. If you come to an angel with a flaming sword, you've gone too far.</u>

A sampling from Moses' suggestion box:

"I realize you're a man, Moses, but how about we stop at the next gas station and ask for directions?"

"I said, 'Turn left at the canyon.' But would you listen to me? Nooo!"

"I think I dropped my money pouch in the Red Sea. Can we go back?"

"Moses, don't you think it's time someone checked your map for a misprint?"

"Don't get me wrong, Moses. I appreciate God's providence, but we've been eating manna for *thirty-eight years!* Can't you find a nice burger joint or something?"

A sampling from Moses' suggestion box (the youth response):

"Are we there yet?"

"Yo dude, that Red Sea thing was cool! Can we do that again?"

"Don't get me wrong, Big Guy. I love every one of these millions of people. But I need my space, man!"

"It's the music, Moses. I mean, c'mon . . . harps? Every night it's harps. Can't we bring in a bass or something?"

"Are we there yet?"

OFFICIAL NOTICE

All restaurants in Egypt, including Pharaoh's Kitchen,
will be closed until further notice
for the following health code violations:

___X___ Water turned to blood
___X___ Frogs (other than those on menu)
___X___ Workers with lice
___X___ Flies
___X___ Unsafe beef
___X___ Workers with unsightly boils
___X___ Hail damage
___X___ Locusts
___X___ Insufficient lighting

Signed:

Moses, Aaron,
and the "Let My People go"
Committee

Remarks overheard the day
God made the sun stand still
for Joshua:

"I thought I told you
to change the battery on the sundial."

"I thought I told *you*
to change the battery on the sundial."

"I thought I told *you*
to change the battery on the sundial."

New Rules of Conduct

FROM: The Creator

TO: The World via Moses

RULES:

1. Thou shalt have no other gods before Me.
2. Thou shalt not make unto thee any graven image.
3. Thou shalt not take the name of the Lord thy God in vain.
4. Thou shalt honor the Sabbath day to keep it holy.
5. Thou shalt honor thy father and thy mother.
6. Thou shalt not kill.
7. Thou shalt not commit adultery.
8. Thou shalt not steal.
9. Thou shalt not bear false witness.
10. Thou shalt not covet.

*Please be advised: these rules *are* etched in stone.

Coroner's remark at the scene of Elijah's translation:

"All right, let's go through this one more time.
I'm here to pick up the body of Elijah.
Now, where'd you say it went?"

A Baby Shower (and 90th Birthday Party) for Sarah

Day:	Saturday
Time:	2:00 PM
Color:	Blue (God says it's a boy!)
Party Theme:	Ripley's "Believe It or Not"
Given By:	The Chosen People's Senior Group

Gift Ideas:	For Baby	For Sarah
	pureed foods	pureed foods
	bib	bib
	gum ointment	gum ointment
	walker	walker
	bed with rails	bed with rails

A Funny Thing Happened...

Bumper stickers for the ark:

I BRAKE FOR MT. ARARAT.

TWO OF EVERY KIND OF ANIMAL ON BOARD

GOD'S CHILDREN AREN'T PERFECT, BUT WE'RE AFLOAT.

IF YOU CAN READ THIS, THANK YOUR SWIM TEACHER.

More bumper stickers
for the ark:

HOW AM I BOATING?
CALL 1-800-ISHOULDHAVELISTENEDTONOAH

GOT LAND?

GOD . . . THE ORIGINAL PROMISE KEEPER

What the lions might
have said to each other
after Daniel was thrown into
their den and God sent
an angel to lock their jaws:

"Sure he looks good, Alice, but for some reason,
I just feel like a salad tonight."

"Doesn't King Nebuchadnezzar know we're trying to cut down
on our prophet intake?"

"Well, I hope you're happy, Harold. My mouth is finally frozen shut!"

"I know it goes against all my natural instincts,
but just this once, I'm passing on dessert."

"Forget him, Martha. Let's play Frisbee!"

JACOB'S OUTDOOR CAFÉ

"We're Open When You're Hungry!"

Today's Menu
Hot Pottage

Dress code strictly enforced.
No sandals.
No birthright.
NO SERVICE!

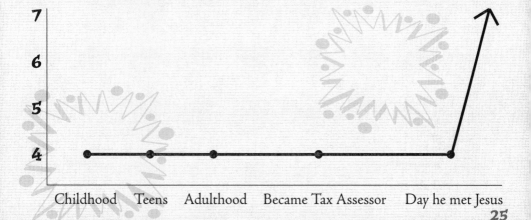

David's Top Ten Countdown

10. Psalm 27

9. Psalm 139

8. Psalm 8

7. Psalm 16

6. Psalm 119 (long-playing)

5. Psalm 108

4. Psalm 117 (jingle)

3. Psalm 100

2. Psalm 1

1. Psalm 23 (topping the charts 3,000 years running)

Why Moses could never have lived in a resort community.

Remarks overheard during
Egypt's plague of flies:

"You left the screen door open *again*,
didn't you, Abigail?"

"Waiter, I think there are 4,000 flies in my soup."

"Where are all those frogs now that we need them, huh?"

"Just how many pounds do these 'No-Pest Strips' hold anyway?"

"All I know, Omar, is you can't have a beauty contest
when the contestants are drawing this many flies!"

Advantages of being
the first people on earth:

1. You can take a shower without the phone ever ringing.
2. You can get your pick of parking spaces at the mall.
3. No lines at the Department of Motor Vehicles.
4. The ATM always has money.
5. You don't have to worry about unexpected company dropping in.
6. Everything in the "Lost and Found" is yours.
7. No junk mail.
8. The remote stays right where you left it.
9. There's no need for "call waiting."
10. No in-laws.

Disadvantages of being the first people on earth:

1. There's no wait at the dentist's office.
2. The IRS has only you to audit.
3. No one replies to your e-mail.
4. Nobody comes to your Tupperware parties.
5. All your mail comes back to you.
6. Shopping isn't much of a challenge.
7. Doing the wave at football games is not that impressive.
8. There are no neighbors to whom to send door-to-door salesmen.
9. Yard sales are boring. It's all your own stuff.
10. You have no family history on which to blame your eccentricities.

Job's Christmas Letter

Dear Friends and Family,

I realize this isn't the usual uplifting Christmas letter. In fact, I don't have much good to report at all. First, our camels were stolen, then our oxen. No insurance, of course. The Chaldeans slew all of our servants, too. So much for the Welcome Wagon in these parts. But that's not the worst of it. Our sons and daughters were partying at my eldest son's home when a big wind came up and blew the house in, killing them all. You probably read about it in the paper. Then, just when I thought things couldn't get any worse, I woke up one morning and discovered my entire body was covered from head to toe with unsightly boils. I've tried every ointment on the market, but nothing has helped.

My wife has tried her best to hold up under all this adversity, but even she told me to just, "curse God and die."

But I didn't listen. Instead, I decided to trust Him, for He's never failed me yet. And who knows what the future has in store. God could bless me with more blessings than I can imagine. I could get everything back seven fold. Why, next year's letter could be filled with the best news of my life! But even if it isn't, one thing's for sure, God is always faithful to His children!

So, how was your year?

Yours truly,

Job

Top five things Moses could have used in the wilderness:

1. A compass
2. Five hundred thousand bunion cushions
3. A compass
4. One million WWMD
   (What Would Moses Do) bracelets
5. A compass

Interpreters Needed Immediately!

All Languages!
Don't Delay! Apply Today!

TOWER OF BABEL CONSTRUCTION COMPANY

A Funny Thing Happened...

Memo from Jonah to God:

What part of "NO" don't You understand?

Memo from God to Jonah:

What part of "GO" don't *you* understand?

John the Baptist's Shopping List

Locusts
Honey
~~Frosted Flakes~~   Locusts
~~Twinkies~~   Honey
~~Peanut Butter~~   Locusts
~~Orange Juice~~   Honey
~~Fig Newtons~~   Locusts
Locusts
Honey

Goliath's Tombstone

Here lies Goliath.
How big he had grown
'Til he took on our God
And then really got stoned.

Methuselah's Birthday Party Invitation

It's that time again!

You are cordially invited to attend a 969th birthday celebration.

FOR: Methuselah (AKA "Junior")

DATE: Friday

TIME: 7:00 PM

WHERE: The Home for the Really, Really Aged

SPECIAL INSTRUCTIONS: Whatever you do, don't shout "SURPRISE!"

Refreshments will be provided.

BYOT (Bring Your Own Teeth).

FYI!

The questionable land sale incident of Ananias and Sapphira
will not be referred to as "Tithe-gate."

Bumper Stickers God Might Have:

MY SON WALKS ON WATER.

MY BOY RAISES THE DEAD.

MY CHILD'S PERFECT

MY SON DIED FOR YOUR HONOR STUDENT.

Accounts Receivable

Debtor: The Unmerciful Servant

Lender: The King

Amount Due: 10,000 talents

Recommendation: Debtor deserves prison.

Credit Arrangements: Debtor has begged for mercy.

Despite recommendations by King's accountant, entire debt has been forgiven.

Accounts Receivable

Debtor: Fellow Servant

Lender: The Unmerciful Servant

Amount Due: 100 pence

Recommendation: Debtor deserves prison.

Credit Arrangements: Debtor has begged for mercy.

                     Despite pleas, no mercy has been
                     granted. Debtor thrown into prison.
                     Let the worm pay!

NOTICE FROM THE KING'S ACCOUNTANT:

New Credit Arrangements for Unmerciful Servant:
Due to the Unmerciful Servant's failure to show mercy
to his fellow servant, original debt has been reinstated.
Debtor will be thrown into prison. Let the unforgiving
worm pay!

Remember our motto: "Mercy . . . don't leave home
without it."

Bethsaida Eye Clinic

A Medical Corporation

E	T
COB	HAN
XFRN	KYOU
SWTVP	JESUS
OAUYBR	CHRIST!

| Normal eye chart. | Eye chart as seen by the blind man at Bethsaida after Jesus healed him. |

Memorial Service

FOR: Lot's wife

DATE: This Saturday

TIME: Dusk

WHERE: The hill just above the ruins of Sodom

Please come and help us remember this pillar of our community.

Why was the feeding of the five thousand with one little boy's lunch of five loaves and two fish an even greater miracle?

1. It was the last banquet on record that didn't serve chicken.

2. Over five thousand were fed, and no one got stuck doing the dishes.

3. All that fish, and, as far as we know, not one person asked for tartar sauce.

4. Thousands of kids didn't have to eat their vegetables that day.

5. No one choked on a fish bone.

6. A banquet for five thousand and the servers didn't demand a 20-percent tip.

7. There's no record of anyone taking cuts in line.

8. It was the first all-you-can-eat buffet without a single macaroni dish.

Jericho's neighbors make the best of a bad situation.

Missing Person Report

JONAH

Missing for two days. Last seen on a ship to
Tarshish before storm. Could be in belly of big fish.
Check your catch. If found, notify
Ninevah Missions Team immediately.

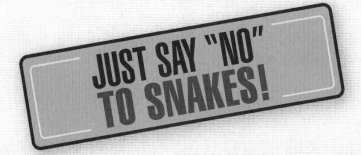

If Eve Had a
Bumper Sticker:

JUST SAY "NO"
TO SNAKES!

If Adam Had a Bumper Sticker:

Special "Top Secret" Orders

From: Gideon

To: All soldiers of Israel

As you know, men, we stand on the threshold of a great battle. The Midianite army numbers into the hundreds of thousands. There are only thirty-two thousand of us. No doubt you have heard by now that I gave the order for any soldier who was afraid to go home. That cut us down to ten thousand men. Then, I watched you men as you drank from the river. Any man who put his head to the water instead of keeping watch with his eyes, I sent home, too.

That leaves us with about three hundred men. Now, I realize some of you might be thinking that I'm suffering from battle fatigue, but I assure you I'm just obeying orders from my Superior Officer. Now—concerning our choice of weapons. We won't be using any this time. We're going to take pitchers, torches, and some trumpets. I know, I know, it's a bit of a *different* approach. I'll tell you all about it at the meeting tonight. But don't worry. God's on our side, and the last time I checked our war records, He hasn't lost a battle yet!

Bestsellers Throughout History:

Gone with the Rain
Written by Noah

Men are from Dust, Women are from Ribs
Written by Adam

I'm O.K., You're History: The Story of Goliath
Written by David

A Tale of Two Cities: The Sodom and Gomorrah Story
Written by Lot

Little Men
Written by the ten spies who went into the land of Canaan
and brought back a report full of fear

A Funny Thing Happened...

The Raven
Written by Elijah

Hamlet
Written by the Prodigal Son

Twenty Thousand Leagues Under the Sea
Written by the Egyptian Army pursuing Moses

"Moses, you're just no fun to play with!"

**Conversations overheard
in Noah's neighbors' homes:**

"I've given you the best years of my life, Harold, and you never built *me* a boat like that."

"We've got him now, Mable! He's violated the two-pet minimum in our Homeowners' Association rules."

"I don't know why he can't just build a regular tool shed like everyone else."

"Look at that Noah. He's there working on that ark from sunup to sundown, and you can't even mow our lawn."

"This is the last time we buy in the suburbs, Agnes. I tell ya, they let every kind of nut live out here."

A Funny Thing Happened...

An Entry from Jonah's Journal:

DAY #3 Bored. Nothing much has changed. Still here in the belly of a big fish. I don't remember reading about this in that Tarshish travel brochure. Excuse my writing, it's dark and the ride tends to get a bit bumpy at times. Have no idea where my luggage is. Haven't eaten in three days. Hate sushi. Never should have run from God. Big mistake. Too late now, non-refundable ticket. But wait! Fish getting ready to sneeze. This could be my ticket outta here! If it works, see you in Nineveh! After *this*, how bad could it be?

The Ten Foolish Virgins' Shopping List:

1. Wedding present

2. Wrapping paper

3. Tissue

4. Ribbon

5. Congratulations card

6. ~~Oil~~ (I think we're got enough.)

Wilderness Café

MENU: Manna

Fresh each morning.

Positively no "to go" boxes
(except for the day before the Sabbath).

Cost: Free to all who will trust in God's provision.

Canaan Family Clinic

Patient Analysis

Patient Names:	Reuben, Simeon, Levi, Judah, Zebulun, Issachar, Dan, Naphtali, Gad, and Asher
Diagnosis:	Acute sibling rivalry

REPORT: During a session with the above-named patients, I observed that the subjects were intensely jealous of a younger brother named Joseph. On the surface, it would seem that a multi-colored coat given to Joseph by the subjects' father has triggered this negative emotion, but I'm afraid the problem may go far deeper. During the session, one brother made a vague reference to having thrown Joseph into a pit, then later selling him into slavery. While the subject may very well be delusional, I sense that he may be telling the truth.

Unfortunately, without solid proof, my doctor/client privilege prohibits me from notifying authorities. It is my recommendation, therefore, that these brothers seek long-term counseling, or better yet, their brother's forgiveness. Perhaps someday, Joseph will have the opportunity and the heart to forgive them. Only time will tell.

FEE: The usual group rate.

FYI

The story of Jacob's Ladder
contains no reference to The Home Depot.

Knock-Knock Joke

Knock, knock.
Who's there?

Jehoshaphat.
Jehoshaphat who?

Jehoshaphat door open so I can come in!

What the first sojourners
might have said when they
came upon what had been the
mighty wall of Jericho:

"Now, this is why there really have to be some ground rules for youth lock-ins."

"And I thought my two-year-old grandson was destructive!"

"I always said they should have just put up chain link."

"Well, I guess this solves our 'how are we going to get into Jericho' dilemma."

"I don't know, but if you ask me, I'd say they tried taking on Somebody they shouldn't have!"

Memorandum

TO: Wife #548

FROM: King Solomon

MESSAGE: Look, sweetie, how many times do I have to tell you—I'm sorry about forgetting our anniversary. But cut me some slack here, will ya? I've got a *thousand* wives! You think it's easy remembering all those anniversary dates?!

OFFICIAL NOTICE

FROM: King Herod

TO: People of Judea

My dear subjects: A young baby has been born in our midst who, it is rumored, is destined to be a king. I can't tell you how excited I am to hear this wonderful news! (NOT!) I truly want to come and worship the baby myself. (YEAH, RIGHT.) If you know the whereabouts of this precious little one, please let me or one of my cabinet members know immediately. We can't wait to honor him. (IF YOU BELIEVE THAT, I'VE GOT SOME TEMPLE JUNK BONDS I'D LOVE TO SELL YOU.) So, please hurry. I'm anxious to know the identity of this new little king! (WHY, I'D KILL TO KNOW HIS IDENTITY!)

I remain your humble leader (WHO HAS NO INTENTION OF EVER GIVING UP THE THRONE!),

King Herod

Found in Goliath's Trash Can:

SLINGSHOT DEFENSE COURSE

Special offer!

Good for a limited time only!

18 shekels—payable in three easy installments.

Think you're tough? Think you're bad?
Well, think again! Military armor is no match for
today's improved slingshot! Protect yourself from
this new form of combat perfected by a shepherd boy
named David. Think about it—you, too, can learn
the ancient art of ducking, weaving, bobbing,
and running for your life.

Don't delay—sign up today!

Class sizes are limited.

20% discount for all giants!

Disclaimer: We assume no responsibility for anyone
foolish enough to take on the God of the Israelites.

REWARD

FROM: Pharaoh

FOR: The capture and return of the Israelite nation

LAST SEEN: Walking through the Red Sea (Don't ask.)

If you have information concerning the disappearance and whereabouts of this vast nation, please contact the "Where'd They Go?" Foundation at 1-800-TELLALL. You need not identify yourself to receive your reward.

Old Testament Anniversary Gift Chart

1st Anniversary	Paper
25th Anniversary	Silver
50th Anniversary	Gold
100th Anniversary	Platinum
150th Anniversary	Plutonium
200th Anniversary	Uranium
300th Anniversary	(Don't worry about it. At this age, you'll both probably forget anyway!)

Peter's thoughts as he walked on the water to Jesus:

"I'm walking on water! I'm walking on water!"

"This is definitely going on my resume."

"Someone really should be videotaping this!"

"Just think what this could save me on future travel expenses."

"I guess this'll teach those other disciples to say,
'That Peter. What does he think he can do? Walk on water?'"

"Look at the size of those waves . . .
Uh, maybe I shouldn't have been so hasty."

"Uh-oh. I'm sinking! Galilee—we have a problem."

"Wait a minute . . . I've got Jesus!
I'll just take hold of His hand."

"It worked! I'm holding on to Jesus' hand and walking on water again!
I'm walking on water and not sinking!"

"Someone really should be videotaping this!"

A Funny Thing Happened...

Note on Daniel's Door:

Spending night in the lions' den. God is with me.
Leave all deliveries on porch—
will be back in the morning.

Daniel

(Political bumper sticker circa 900 BC)

KING SOLOMON'S A WISE GUY!

Martha's "TO DO" List

1. Cook
2. Dust
3. Complain to Jesus about Mary
4. Wash last night's dishes
5. Mop
6. Complain to Jesus about Mary
7. Set table
8. Fill beverage glasses
9. Complain to Jesus about Mary
10. If there's time left over, spend some of it with Jesus.

Mary's "TO DO" List

1. Spend time with Jesus

Common problem
at Lot's dinner table:

How to ask him to "pass the salt."

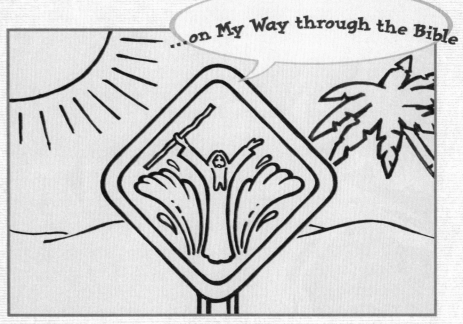

"Moses Crossing."

Jerusalem Police Report

TIME: 1800 Hours

LOCATION: The road to Jericho

CRIME: Assault, robbery

VICTIM: Jewish male (identity, age unknown)

WITNESS ACCOUNT: Witness states victim was beaten and robbed and left by the side of the road. A priest and a Levite passed by victim but refused to get involved. As the "Good Samaritan Law" hasn't been enacted yet, charges cannot be brought against the two at this time. Another stranger, a

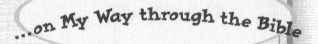

Samaritan, did stop. He lifted the victim onto the back of his own donkey, transported him to the nearest inn for emergency medical treatment and lodging, and picked up expense for same.

PROGNOSIS OF VICTIM: Stable and improving. Needs to continue treatment.

PROGNOSIS OF SOCIETY: Needs more good Samaritans.

Enlistment Application

Name: David

Tour of Duty Requested: Battle with Goliath

Special Talents: Good with slingshot

Songwriting

No fear of giants

Great faith

References: God

Mothers-in-law Are All That!

A FREE Seminar

Special Guest Speaker—Ruth

Having trouble with your mother-in-law? Take heart.
Hope is just a seminar away! Come hear this dynamic speaker as she tells
of her incredible relationship with her mother-in-law, Naomi.
You'll laugh! You'll cry! It'll change your own in-law relationships forever!

Where: Boaz's place

When: Dusk

Admission: FREE!

Lunch will be provided. Sorry, videotaping strictly prohibited.
(You'll have to buy the book.)

What Jacob might have
said when he discovered
he'd been tricked into marrying
Leah, the oldest daughter of
Laban, instead of Rachel,
whom he loved:

"I don't know who did your makeup, Rachel,
but I'd try to get my money back if I were you."

"I knew I should have read those wedding invitations
a little more closely."

"Rachel, either you've really changed or somebody has slipped
something into the reception punch."

One Beloved Lamb. AKA: Lost Sheep.

What Balaam's donkey probably wanted to say after Balaam struck him three times for not going on when an angel of God was blocking the way:

"Look, I've had just about enough of your back-seat driving!"

"Do that again and you're taking the bus!"

"Where's the SPCA when you need 'em, huh?"

"Sorry, pal, but around here angels have the right of way."

Gideon's Army Surplus

ONLY FOUR SHEKELS!!!

Direct from Gideon's battle! The actual pitchers used
by Gideon's army to defeat the Midianites!
(A little Krazy Glue and they're good as new!)
Own a memento from one of the most incredible
battles in history! Don't miss out! Get yours today!

**Torches and trumpets sold separately.

Delilah's Hair Club for Nazirites

For all your hair-care needs.
Ask about our "Samson Special."

Shampoo & Set	1 shekel
Perm	3 shekels
Weave	6 shekels
Haircut	The secret to your strength

*Only your hairdresser knows for sure . . .
and she's telling *everybody*.

Adam's thoughts when he first saw Eve:

"Yeah, but can she cook?"

"There goes the bachelor pad."

"Well, this *used* to be paradise.
Now, I guess I've got to start picking up after myself."

"I don't remember seeing *her* on the animal list."

"Ummm . . . now that's interesting. There's a creature that looks
an awful lot like me . . . only . . . well, different."

"She's nice, but with my luck, she's probably already married."

Jerusalem Ear Clinic

PATIENT'S NAME: Malchus

PATIENT'S STATEMENT: Patient states right ear was cut off by a man named Peter and was then reattached by Jesus of Nazareth.

EXAM RESULTS: Healing verified. Perfect reattachment. No evidence of trauma of any kind. No sutures needed. No symptoms of infection. Hearing range—normal.

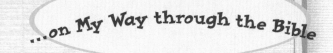

TREATMENT: Irrigate (*we've got to charge him for something*) and release.

RECOMMENDATION: Resume daily activities. Avoid anyone who says, "Lend me your ear."

What the pigs might have thought about the Prodigal Son sharing their pigpen:

"Whose litter does *that* one belong to?"

"I wish he'd clean up a little. He's giving the rest of us a bad name."

"What does he think this is? A 'pen and breakfast'?"

"There goes the neighborhood!"

Book of Manners
by
One Thankful Leper

Foreword:

A general lack of manners seems to characterize today's society. Since Emily Post hasn't been born yet, and Ann Landers is centuries away from penning her first newspaper column, I had no choice but to write a book myself addressing the subject of manners. First of all, let me say that on the day Jesus healed me, I was so happy that I rushed back and thanked Him. To my amazement, however, the other nine who were healed that day went on their way as though miraculous healings happen every day.

They don't, of course. We have taken so many of God's blessings for granted. It is my prayer, that through the pages of this book, those nine lepers, and others who have acted equally as ungrateful to our Lord, will recognize their appalling lack of social graces and see to it that they thank Him daily for His many blessings and miracles!

*Author is happy to use his brand-new hands to autograph book upon request.

What some of the animals on the ark might have commented during their mysterious journey . . . if they could have talked:

"Relax Agnes. It'll be fun. And if it *doesn't* rain, what has it cost us, huh?"

"I just hope Noah separates the two elephants,
or we're all going to sink for sure!"

"I don't know what I'm doing here either, Hank.
I was just following a trail of Kibbles 'n Bits
and the next thing I know, we're going on a cruise!"

"All I know is there are two of each of us.
My guess is it's some kind of new animal dating service."

"This odor is unbearable! Next time, Harry,
we travel on the upper deck or we stay home!"

Paraphrased from Proverbs:

Gossiper—The original heavy meddler.

From the Desk of Saul

Gone to Damascus. Anticipate uneventful trip.
Can't wait to return to same-ol', same-ol'.
You know how I resist change.

Saul

Newest Video Releases

Watch for these new blockbusters coming
to a video store near you!

A Few Good Men—Well, Two Anyway
The story of Joshua and Caleb,
the only two spies who had enough faith to believe God
and go in and take the Promised Land.
Rated G for "Good Report."

A River Runs through Everything
Based on the true-life story of Noah, this movie has it all—
animals, conflict, disaster, and a message of hope.
We don't want to give away the ending,
but can you say "rainbow"?

All about Eve
Screenplay by the Serpent.
The story of the Garden of Eden scandal.
Not recommended. Author is biased, full
of misinformation, and predictable.

More Video Releases

My Best Sister's Wedding

This is the story of Leah and Rachel, as told through the eyes of Rachel. Adored by Jacob, Rachel had to be content with being just a bridesmaid, while her beloved was tricked into marrying her sister.

Not just another chick flick. Guys will love this one, too.

Get Shorty . . . Zaccheus, That Is

Just in time for April 15th, this new release is about a tax collector and his brush with kindness. Not your typical tax film. It's funny, poignant, and a good lesson in keeping your house clean, because you never know who's coming over!

The Egyptian princess' five guesses as to what was in the basket floating in the bulrushes:

1. A salmon traveling upstream in style.

2. Fast food sent from the palace.

3. A note from someone stranded on a deserted island.

4. Fresh towels.

5. An Israelite baby.

Dear Coach Renquist,

Remember how you never picked me for any of the sports teams? Remember how I was always a water boy and how I won the award for most time spent on the bench? Well, I thought you might like to read the enclosed news article.

Shepherd Boy Slays Giant

David, the young shepherd boy we've been hearing so much about, has done it again! This time he has single-handedly—with God's help of course—brought down the mighty Goliath. Using only his slingshot, a skill he says he was forced to perfect in high school when Coach Renquist passed him over for the sports teams, David felled the great giant with one shot. A reception honoring this new town hero will be held at the military recreation hall tomorrow.

Just thought you'd like to know,

David

"Guess we're gonna have the last laugh on ol' Samson
after all, eh, Nebulan?"

They Had Mothers, Too!

SAMSON'S MOM: Your father and I warned you about that woman. Now, look at you. Not only is your strength gone, but those curls! Those beautiful curls!

NOAH'S MOM: I'm not saying your ark isn't nice, Noah. I'm just saying it's a little big for your wood-shop project, don't you think?

JONAH'S MOM: I don't care where you've been for three days, Jonah! You still could have called! And wipe your feet! You're dripping water everywhere!

Notice of Legal Name Change

Former Names: Abram (no last name provided)

Sarai (no last name provided)

New Names: Abraham

Sarah

Reason for Change: Orders from God

Please see that all legal papers, school records, and monogrammed bath towels reflect the above name changes.

Judge Solomon's Court

You think Judge Judy knows her stuff?
Today on *Judge Solomon's Court*, two mothers both claim
maternal rights to the same baby. One of the mothers is even
petitioning the court to divide the child in two and give one half
to her and one half to the other mother. Sort of brings new
meaning to the term "shared custody," doesn't it?
What will be Judge Solomon's decision? Come find out!
Plenty of free seats still available!

Dear Mom and Dad,

Remember how I've always loved animals? Well, I'm writing to you from a lions' den here in Babylon. Don't worry, I'm fine. God has shut their mouths so they can't bite me. They're really cute under these circumstances. Not as cute as the puppy I always wanted, but they do make nice pillows.

I'll probably be released tomorrow when King Darius comes and sees that my God has proven Himself yet again to be the one true God. Until then, know that I love you.

Your son,

DANIEL

Weather Report

Sea of Galilee—the raging storm which came up suddenly last night ended just as suddenly when Jesus of Nazareth spoke the words, "Peace, be still." Witnesses reported the winds and waves immediately calmed, and it was smooth sailing from then on. Who says, "Everyone talks about the weather, but no one does anything about it"?

A Funny Thing Happened...

Balaam's Amazing Animal Tales!

Date: Tonight
Time: Dusk
Where: Outside main tent

Hear the first-hand account of Balaam's incredible donkey tale! Listen as he describes how God allowed his donkey to talk to him, warning him that there was an angel in their path. This is NOT just another publicity stunt. All facts have been substantiated. Come hear for yourself! Seating is limited, so come early. Donkeys invited, too. No guarantees, but we're hoping Balaam's donkey might even share a few words.

Rules for Life

Rule #1 Love the Lord your God with all your heart and with all your soul and with all your mind.

Rule #2 Love your neighbor as yourself.

Rule #3 Refer to Rules 1 & 2.

From the Pen of the Prodigal Son:

Dear Dad,

This isn't easy for me to write. Life hasn't been going very well for me lately. First, there was the time I . . . , no, I'd better start with the other night when . . . , wait, I've gotta first tell you about the . . . , oh never mind. I'll just tell you in person. I'm coming home.

See you soon,

Your Prodigal Son

You're Invited to a Party!

WHAT: The greatest homecoming celebration in history!

FOR: My prodigal son

WHEN: As soon as I see him coming up the road!

REFRESHMENTS: Fatted calf and all the trimmings! (Positively no take-out or frozen foods.)

PARTY THEME: Forgiveness/Restoration

DRESS: Come as you are. All are welcome!

RSVP: The Father

Forgiveness Audit

You, _____ (fill in name), are hereby notified that under the forgiveness recommendations set forth in the Holy Scriptures, namely that we are to forgive one another 7 X 70 (equivalent to 490 times), you are now at 480 and have only 10 free passes remaining.

Signed, _____

Lifeguards Wanted!

Apply Today!

IMMEDIATE PLACEMENT: Community under water after twenty days of solid rain with no letup in sight. Applicant must be excellent swimmer, preferably able to catch up to the ark that floated off some days ago.

BENEFITS: All the fish you can eat, opportunity to tan on duty, and high-rise housing provided . . . for a few more days at least.

Get-Out-of-Jail-Free Card

This card entitles the bearers,
Paul and Silas, to get out of jail free
upon the presentation of their faith.

Walk-a-thon for Lame Man at Bethesda

(to raise money for new shoes)

Meet at city gates at dawn.

All gifts are tax deductible.

NOTE: Thanks to Jesus' miraculous touch, the lame man will be doing all of his own walking.

Philistine-Gram

Need more time. Samson close to revealing secret
to strength. Not ropes. Not cords. Could be hair.
Will let you know.

Delilah

Dear Adam,

Went for a walk. Cain's been picking on Abel
all day. If he doesn't get a handle on this jealousy
thing soon, someone's going to get hurt.
Do something.

Love,
Eve

Announcing the Newest Addition to the Royal Family!

NAME: Baby Moses

BIRTHDATE: Unknown. Found in a basket floating down the river.

ADOPTIVE MOTHER: The Princess, Daughter of Pharaoh

WHAT HE WANTS TO DO WHEN HE GROWS UP:
Cross the Red Sea on dry ground. (Children . . . what will they think of next?)

FOR SALE

One tower to Heaven, never used.
Building permits revoked by higher authority.
Finish at your own risk.

See ROCK (OF AGES) CITY!

See the only city built on the Rock, Jesus Christ!
Streets of gold, gates of pearl!
Must see to believe.
Limited time only!
Taking reservations NOW!
Make yours today!

FOR SALE

Cheap! Beautiful four-bedroom, two-bath house, built on sand! Two-story, but hurry! Could be one-story if it sinks any more! By appointment only.

CONTACT FOOLISH BUILDER AT 1-800-DUMBMOV.

SCOREBOARD

Goliath	0
God of David	1
Lions	0
God of Daniel	1
Flames	0
God of Shadrach, Meshach, and Abednego	1

Pharaoh	0
God of Moses	1
Baal	0
God of Elijah	1
Undefeated Champion:	God of Eternity

Dear Mom and Dad,

Hope you liked those 4 dozen hot cross buns I sent you last week, and the 12 dozen cookies I sent the week before, and the 18 pound cakes I sent yesterday, and the 125 homemade biscuits I'm sending today.

I guess you're wondering what all this is about, especially here in the middle of a famine. Well, remember how I told you that I had only enough oil and meal to make a little loaf of bread for Junior and me to eat, then we were surely going to die of starvation?

Well, while I was out gathering sticks a few weeks ago, a prophet named Elijah came to the gate of the city and asked me for a cup of water. Then he asked for a piece of bread, too. I told him that I had only enough for Junior and me, but he said to make a loaf for him first and I would have oil and flour until the famine is over. Trusting him, I did as he asked and guess what? I've got so much oil and flour now that I'm thinking about opening up my own bakery!

Just thought you'd like to know.

Your loving daughter

Temple Guard Log Sheet

RE: Graffiti on wall

REPORTED BY: King Belshazzar

INCIDENT: At approximately 1800 hours, witnesses reported seeing a hand mysteriously writing the following words on the temple wall: "Mene, Mene, Tekel, Upharsin." Not your usual graffiti, so the prophet Daniel was summoned to interpret. Daniel told King Belshazzar that because of his pride and disobedience, God wrote on the wall to warn him that his kingdom would be given to the Medes and the Persians.

DEPARTMENT PLAN OF ACTION: Wall writing by God is not a crime. Charges are dropped. Case closed.

PERSONAL PLAN OF ACTION: Cash in 401K and move to another jurisdiction. A king who doesn't know enough to obey God isn't safe to work for. Signing off. End of watch.

CATCH OF THE DAY!!!

FISHERMEN: Simon Peter, James, and John.

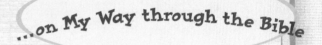

WEIGHT OF CATCH: More than their nets could hold.

SPECIAL BAIT: All they did was cast their nets
where Jesus told them to in the water.

FISH FRY AND FAREWELL TONIGHT AT SUNDOWN
Simon Peter, James, and John have decided
to leave everything and follow Jesus.
With this catch, can't say that we blame them!

Jordan River Water District

RE: Report filed by Elisha, the prophet, regarding floating axe head.

WATER ANALYSIS: Water in the Jordan River has been tested, and results reveal nothing that would make an iron axe head float.

IMPRESSIONS: A miracle.

PUBLIC WARNING: No public warning need be issued. The Jordan River water is still good, but the God of Elisha is better.

Elijah's Tipping Chart

Self-service — 10% or more for busboy

Served by waiter — 15-20%, depending on service

Served by ravens — 100% commitment to God for His amazing providence

A Funny Thing Happened...
THIS SEAT SAVED FOR ZACCHEUS. BE RIGHT BACK.
APPEARING TODAY—JESUS OF NAZARETH.

Appearing Today!

Jesus of Nazareth in person!!!

Come see what all the buzz is about!

Children welcome!
(If anyone tells you differently, tell them Jesus said it's okay.)

God's Daily Planner:

Creation Week-at-a-Glance

Day One: Create light. Divide darkness and light. Call the darkness "night" and the light "day."

Day Two: Make the sky. Call the sky "heaven."

Day Three: Form oceans and lakes so that bodies of dry ground will appear. Make trees and bushes.

Day Four: Set sun and moon and stars in place.

Day Five: Create birds and fish.

Day Six: Create animals and man and woman.

Day Seven: Good job if I say so Myself.
Believe I'll take a little rest!

Dress Code

The following dress code will now be in effect for the duration of your life.

Uniform: Whole armor of God (belt of truth, breastplate of righteousness, shield of faith, helmet of salvation, sword of the Spirit, shoes of peace)

The uniform is free and will be provided to anyone who requests it. Those choosing not to wear the approved uniform are hereby warned that they are placing their safety, and perhaps the safety of those around them, at great risk.

Remember:
No belt of truth?
No shield of faith?
Of no real service.

Paraphrased from Proverbs:

Bearing false witness—giving the truth stretch marks.

Bestseller List

1. The Holy Bible
2. The Holy Bible
3. The Holy Bible
4. The Holy Bible
5. The Holy Bible
6. The Holy Bible
7. The Holy Bible
8. The Holy Bible
9. The Holy Bible
10. The Holy Bible

Read any good books lately?

About the Author

Martha Bolton is an Emmy-nominated writer for Bob Hope and the author of more than thirty humorous books. She also writes for Ann Jillian, Phyllis Diller, Mark Lowry, Kathy Troccoli, and others.

Known as "The Cafeteria Lady" to her many *Brio* magazine fans, Martha has also written numerous youth devotionals, including *Never Ask Delilah for a Trim . . . and Other Good Advice*.

Martha is the winner of two International Angel awards and has received a Dove Award nomination for the children's musical *A Lamb's Tale*.

Martha's positive take on life makes her a popular speaker for both the secular and religious markets. She is married to three-times retired LAPD sergeant, Russ Bolton, currently Security Manager for CBS Studios in Hollywood, California. The Boltons have three sons.

Additional copies of this book are available from your local bookstore.

If you have enjoyed this book, or if it has impacted your life, we would like to hear from you.

Please contact us at:

Honor Books
Department E
P.O. Box 55388
Tulsa, Oklahoma 74155

Or by e-mail at info@honorbooks.com